When Mommy Needs A Time·out

written by
Valarie Pearce

illustrated by
Meredith Johnson

FROM THE LIBRARY OF
VP
VALARIE PEARCE

For my mother, Mrs. Annie Doakes,
who always believes in me.
And, to Iman and Raven,
you are true gifts to my life.
Time-outs on me! In Hawaii… Someday.

• • •

When Mommy Needs A Time-out

Text copyright © 2009 Valarie Pearce
Illustrations © 2009 Meredith Johnson

•

All rights reserved. No part of this book may be
reproduced in any form or by any electronic or mechanical means,
including information storage and retrieval systems,
without written permission from the publisher.

•

Library of Congress Cataloging-in-Publication Data
Pearce, Valarie
When Mommy Needs A Timeout / by Valarie Pearce
Illustrated by Meredith Johnson / Book & Cover design by Cathe Physioc

•

Summary: Two little girls discover that being helpful
is the best way to relieve their mother of a stressful day.

ISBN 9780984311156
[1. Family Life – Fiction   2. Parenting – Fiction 3. Problem Solving – Fiction]

Book design by Cathe Physioc
in collaboration with Valarie Pearce, Author, IR Publishing
Title font: Myriad Tilt / Text font: Phizzies Thin Dot, designer / Cathe Physioc

•

Printed in the United States of America

•

Lightning Source Inc. an Ingram Content Group,
1246 Heil Quaker Blvd., La Vergne, TN USA 37086
in conjunction with : IR Publishing, www.imarapublishing.com

•

Revised Edition, 2012

IR
PUBLISHING
Summit

Hi!

My name is Jetta
and this is my little sister,
Gracie.

At the cash register in every store,
my sister and I always know the score:

Stand still and behave
while Mommy makes an exchange.

But this particular day,
That just wasn't the case;

for my sister had an emergency,
and it needed attention immediately.

What it was, I'll bet you can guess;
and in the end, it was quite a mess...

hands waving
up
and
down,

feet hopping
side to side,

eyes rolling back and forth.

She could not hold it
for much more!

Oh no!

She's really gotta go!

Mommy!

Mooommyy!!!

But Mommy did not use her listening ears,

...so there was an accident.

I stood and watched, then quietly pronounced,
"I think someone needs a time-out."

We rushed from the store
and out into the parking lot
we poured.

Trying to hurry and holding our hands,
Mommy broke a most important
safety rule and command...
no stopping or looking or listening first.

She barely missed toppling our neighbor, Mr. Bert.

It was so sad,
and boy, was he mad!

From my car seat, I inserted quietly,
"Someone needs a time-out to think."

We arrived at the soccer field just in time!
The big game was starting
and we were ready to shine.

Kicking and passing and one score as well,
our team was having fun and doing quite swell.

But then it happened,
though I hoped it wouldn't.
Mommy was loud when she really shouldn't.

Finally, the referee said, "That's it, out PLEASE!"
It's obvious to me.
Mommy needs a time-out, indeed!

We left the game and continued our day;
stopping for take-out dinner on the way.
When we got home and started to empty the car,
Mommy was on the phone and deep in thought

juggling
and walking,
wiggling
and talking.

Yum yum
Chicken
BARN

And, then...
SPLAT!
What a sound!

There was our dinner all over the ground
in yellow, red, green and brown.

I won't say it to her, but she'd say it to me,

"Young lady, you need a time-out immediately!"

But all those things, they weren't so bad,
until the ultimate accident, and it really was sad!

While

cooking

and cleaning

and homework too...

I knew she didn't mean it, but what a thing to do!

For Filbert was my sister's best buddy from birth,
and when Mommy broke him,
my sister cried for all it was worth!

And then it hit me!
All day it was true.

Mommy did need a time-out.

And **helping** her would
be a nice thing to do.

So tip-toeing

and sneaking

and squealing too,

My sister and I
found just the
right things to do.

And Mommy, so comfy and happy
with her favorite book,

said, "Thank you."
And a time-out she took.

CPSIA information can be obtained
at www.ICGtesting.com
Printed in the USA
BVHW052221190720
584048BV00003B/49